remember

PEARL HARBOR

remember

PEARL HARBOR

American and Japanese Survivors
Tell Their Stories

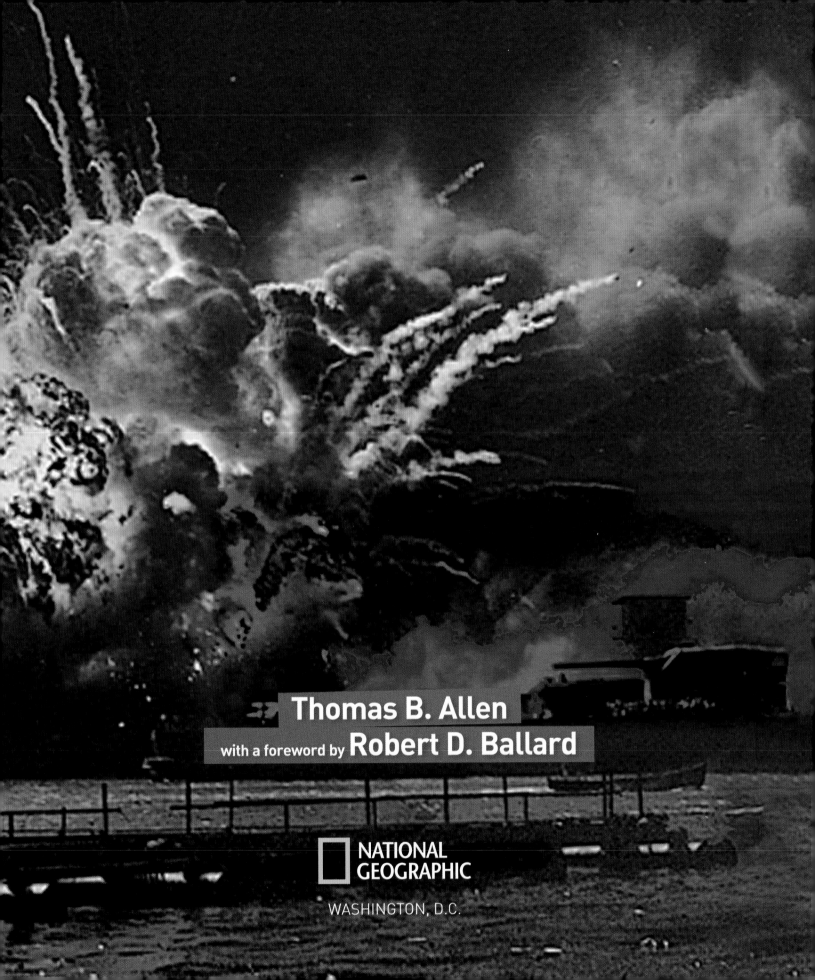

Thomas B. Allen
with a foreword by **Robert D. Ballard**

NATIONAL
GEOGRAPHIC

WASHINGTON, D.C.

To my grandchildren. May they always live in peace.

STAFF FOR THIS BOOK
Suzanne Patrick Fonda, *Project Editor*
Bea Jackson, *Art Director, Children's Books*
Gerry Greaney, Greaney Design, *Designer*
Callie Broaddus, *Associate Designer*
Lori Epstein, *Senior Photo Editor*
Sadie Quarrier, *Illustrations Editor*
Meredith C. Wilcox, *Illustrations Assistant*
Carl Mehler, *Director of Maps*
Matt Chwastyk, National Geographic Maps,
     and Martin S. Walz, *Map Research and Production*
Jennifer Emmett, *Associate Editor*
Paige Towler, *Editorial Assistant*
Lewis R. Bassford, *Production Manager*
Jennifer Hoff, *Manager, Production Services*

PUBLISHED BY THE NATIONAL GEOGRAPHIC SOCIETY
Gary E. Knell, *President and CEO*
John M. Fahey, *Chairman of the Board*
Melina Gerosa Bellows, *Chief Education Officer*
Declan Moore, *Chief Media Officer*
Hector Sierra, *Senior Vice President and General Manager, Book Division*

SENIOR MANAGEMENT TEAM, KIDS PUBLISHING AND MEDIA
Nancy Laties Feresten, *Senior Vice President;* Jennifer Emmett, *Vice
President, Editorial Director, Kids Books;* Julie Vosburgh Agnone, *Vice
President, Editorial Operations;* Rachel Buchholz, *Editor and Vice President,* NG Kids *magazine;* Michelle Sullivan, *Vice President, Kids Digital;*
Eva Absher-Schantz, *Design Director;* Jay Sumner, *Photo Director;*
Hannah August, *Marketing Director;* R. Gary Colbert, *Production Director*

DIGITAL
Anne McCormack, *Director;* Laura Goertzel, Sara Zeglin, *Producers;*
Jed Winer, *Special Projects Assistant;* Emma Rigney, *Creative Producer;*
Brian Ford, *Video Producer;* Bianca Bowman, *Assistant Producer;*
Natalie Jones, *Senior Product Manager*

Text is set in ITC New Baskerville

The National Geographic Society is one of the world's largest nonprofit scientific and educational organizations. Founded in 1888 to "increase and diffuse geographic knowledge," the Society's mission is to inspire people to care about the planet. It reaches more than 400 million people worldwide each month through its official journal, *National Geographic,* and other magazines; National Geographic Channel; television documentaries; music; radio; films; books; DVDs; maps; exhibitions; live events; school publishing programs; interactive media; and merchandise. National Geographic has funded more than 10,000 scientific research, conservation, and exploration projects and supports an education program promoting geographic literacy.

For more information, please visit nationalgeographic.com,
call 1-800-NGS LINE (647-5463), or write to the following address:

NATIONAL GEOGRAPHIC SOCIETY
1145 17th Street N.W.
Washington, D.C. 20036-4688 U.S.A.

Visit us online at nationalgeographic.com/books

For librarians and teachers: ngchildrensbooks.org

More for kids from National Geographic: kids.nationalgeographic.com

For information about special discounts for bulk purchases, please contact
National Geographic Books Special Sales: ngspecsales@ngs.org

**National Geographic supports K–12 educators with ELA Common Core
Resources. Visit natgeoed.org/commoncore for more information.**

Printed in Hong Kong
15/THK/1

ACKNOWLEDGMENTS
Special thanks to Jack Green, U.S. Naval Historical Center; Daniel A.
Martinez, historian; Yukako Yamamoto Seltzer, translator; Junko Taguchi,
project coordinator in Japan; Tria Thalman, National Geographic
Television; and all the survivors without whose cooperation this book
would not have been possible.

The Library of Congress cataloged the 2001 edition as follows:
Allen, Thomas B.
     Remember Pearl Harbor : American and Japanese survivors tell their
stories / by Thomas B. Allen ; foreword by Robert D. Ballard.
     p. cm.
Includes bibliographical references and index.
ISBN 0-7922-6690-0
     1. Pearl Harbor (Hawaii), Attack on, 1941--Juvenile literature.
2.Pearl Harbor (Hawaii), Attack on, 1941—Personal narratives—Juvenile
literature. [1. Pearl Harbor (Hawaii), Attack on, 1941.
2. World War, 1939–1945—Personal narratives.]—I. Title.
     D767.92 .A714 2001
     940.54'26–dc21
                                        2001000796

2015 paperback edition ISBN: 978-1-4263-2248-8
2015 reinforced library edition ISBN: 978-1-4263-2353-9

PHOTO CREDITS
NA = National Archives; NGS = National Geographic Society;
NHC = U.S. Naval Historical Center; NPS = National Park Service

Front cover, NA #80-G-19948; 1, Stuart N. Hedley; 2-3, NHC; 5 (up),
Courtesy Yuji Akamatsu; 5 (up center), NA #80-G-19948; 5 (low center), NA
#80-G-32420; 5 (low), Tria Thalman; 6, Priit Vesilind, NGS; 7, Royalty Free/
Corbis; 8, From the collection of Stanley Weintraub; 11, Hulton-Deutsch
Collection/Corbis; 13, U.S.S. *Arizona* Memorial, NPS; 14, M. Nakamura;
15 (both), Courtesy Yuji Akamatsu; 16, Bettmann/Corbis; 17, NA #80-
G-71198; 18, NA #80-G-351875; 19, Courtesy Kichiji Dewa; 22, NHC; 24
(map), DEM source: Royce A. Jones, GDSI, Hawaii; 24, U.S.S. *Arizona*
Memorial, NPS; 26, Courtesy Haruo Yoshino; 27, NHC; 28, NA #80-G-19948;
29, NA #80-G-182252; 30 (up), Courtesy The National Museum of the
Pacific War, Texas Parks & Wildlife Department; 30 (low), NA #80-G-
17016; 31, NHC; 32, NHC; 33, Courtesy Russell Reetz; 34, U.S.S. *Arizona*
Memorial, NPS; 36, Courtesy Charles Christensen; 37, NA #80-G-40056;
38, Courtesy George Smith; 39, U.S.S. *Arizona* Memorial, NPS; 40,
Corbis; 41 (up), U.S.S. *Arizona* Memorial, NPS; 41 (low), Courtesy Clark
Simmons; 42, Courtesy Anna Carson; 43, U.S.S. *Arizona* Memorial, NPS;
44, NA #80-G-32420; 45, Courtesy Claire Becker; 46, Courtesy Madelyn
Blonskey Knapp; 47 (both), U.S.S. *Arizona* Memorial, NPS; 48, Courtesy
George Smith; 49, NA #80-G-32536; 50, Tria Thalman; 53, David Doubilet;
54, U.S.S. *Arizona* Memorial, NPS; 56 (up), Stuart N. Hedley; 56 (low)
U.S.S. *Arizona* Memorial, NPS; Back cover (clockwise from top left),
Courtesy of Yuji Akamatsu, Clark Simmons, Madelyn Blonskey Knapp,
George Smith, and Kichiji Dewa.

COVER: Ford Island Naval Air Station under Japanese attack

*PAGES 4–5: People enjoy a day of pre–Pearl Harbor
     peace on a sunny Hawaiian beach.*

TITLE PAGE: Flames and smoke erupt from the destroyer U.S.S. Shaw
     during the Japanese attack on Pearl Harbor.

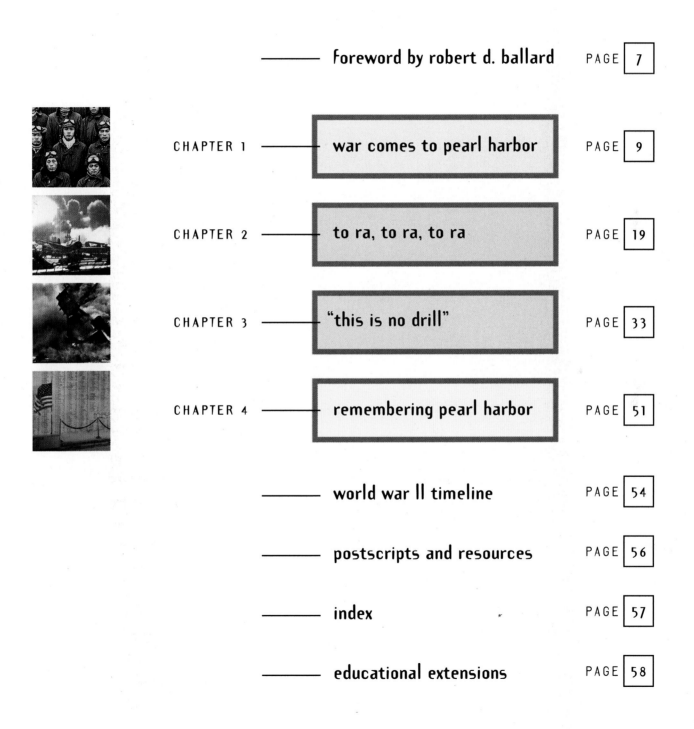

Underwater explorer Robert Ballard (wearing sunglasses) helps ready a robot submarine for launch near the entrance to Pearl Harbor. He is searching for a Japanese midget submarine that was part of the force sent to attack the U.S. Pacific Fleet on December 7, 1941.

Foreword

U.S.S. *Arizona* Memorial, Pearl Harbor

Pearl Harbor means a lot to me as a naval officer. Here, in defeat, the U.S. Navy rose from smoke and flame to fight and win a war. As an underwater explorer, I see the harbor itself as a fascinating place. Under the peaceful waters is a battlefield that still holds secrets of December 7, 1941.

I often have stood at the U.S.S. *Arizona* Memorial, a great white monument that marks the battleship U.S.S. *Arizona,* which still rests where she sank that Sunday morning in 1941. On a wall in the memorial are the names of the 1,177 men who died on the ship.

For the United States, World War II started here at Pearl Harbor. I look at those names, and I think that most people who fought in World War II were teenagers. They lived on a farm in Kansas or were just out of high school in Detroit or were working at the family hardware store in Maine. Then, all of a sudden, they found themselves in a war that would change world history.

Many died in that war, and the U.S.S. *Arizona* Memorial helps us honor and remember those heroes who died for their country. But most of those who fought for America in World War II came back, bringing with them the memories of a terrible war.

Men and women who come back from war are usually called veterans. Men and women who were at Pearl Harbor on December 7, 1941, call themselves survivors. They survived those two hours of bombing and torpedoing that devastated Pearl Harbor and the airfields on Oahu. But the attack did not destroy the spirit of the survivors. They went on to fight and win the war.

In this book we meet some of those American survivors and hear their memories. We also meet some Japanese survivors who share what they remember about the day they attacked Pearl Harbor. Maybe from the stories of these people who once were enemies you can get a better understanding of what happened at Pearl Harbor.

On a recent trip to Hawaii, I took my seven-year-old son Benjamin to the U.S.S. *Arizona* Memorial. I wondered what Pearl Harbor would mean to him. He looked at the names on the wall, and he walked to the round opening in the deck of the monument. Leaning on a rail around the opening, Ben looked down and saw the remains of the *Arizona.* Minutes went by. And more minutes. Finally, I asked, "Ben, what are your thoughts?"

"This is a very special place," he said. "And it's a very sad place."

Yes, it is a sad and special place. It is a place where we remember not just the *Arizona* and Pearl Harbor, but also a world war. And if you remember this war and its cost in human lives and suffering, you will never want another war.

Robert D. Ballard

Ensign Views Midway Battle from Sea
© Gum, Inc.

Dying Captain Carries On
© Gum, Inc.

MacArthur Starts Dash to Australia
© Gum, Inc.

Dutch Kill Sky Troops at Sumatra
© Gum, Inc.

Cards called "Horrors of War" came with bubble gum in prewar and war years. The cards distorted historical events and exaggerated acts by both heroes and enemies. But they lived up to their name, teaching countless American children that World War II was a worldwide horror of death and destruction.

CHAPTER 1

war comes to pearl harbor

There are some days that you will never forget. For Americans who were alive on Sunday, December 7, 1941, that was one of those days. It was the day that Japan attacked Pearl Harbor.

Late in the afternoon of December 7, 1941, I came home from a Boy Scout hike. My mother and father hardly noticed that I had come in. They were sitting on chairs drawn up to the radio, which stood in a corner of the living room. I could tell something big had happened somewhere. The radio usually gave us music and shows. But for the past couple of years, ever since the war started in Europe, the radio also gave us news about the war.

"The Japanese bombed Pearl Harbor," my father told me. His voice was hushed. My mother said nothing. She just looked at me, her 12-year-old son in his Boy Scout uniform, and she looked sad. A long time later, I thought back and knew that she had been wondering whether the war would last until I was old enough to go.

"Where is Pearl Harbor?" I asked.

"In Hawaii," my father said.

I knew that in parts of the world there already was a war. It had started in 1939, when Germany invaded Poland. England and France, as allies of Poland, had declared war on Germany. In the spring of 1940, Germany invaded Belgium, France, the Netherlands, Luxembourg, Denmark, and Norway. I learned about the war mostly by reading our local newspaper and listening to the news on the radio. I also got some ideas from "war cards" that came with bubble gum. The war cards showed a lot of blood and a lot of horror in drawings that were like the drawings in comic books. But there was something real about the war card pictures. They showed me that in war, people were wounded and killed—and not just soldiers and sailors. Civilians, even children, were dying in air raids.

My family lived on the first floor of a two-family house. The family that lived on the second floor had a son in the Army. Hanging in a front window was a little white

The Japanese Empire in World War II

UNION OF SOVIET SOCIALIST REPUBLICS (SOVIET UNION)

ALASKA (U.S.)

Bering Sea

Sea of Okhotsk (U.S.S.R.)

Kamchatka Peninsula

Attu (U.S.)

Kiska

Aleutian Islands

50N

Sakhalin (Japan)

OUTER MONGOLIA

Urga

MANCHUKUO (MANCHURIA) (Japan)

CHINA

Hokkaido

NORTH

40N

CHOSEN (KOREA) (Japan)

Honshu

Sea of Japan

Tokyo

JAPAN

PACIFIC

AFGHANISTAN

Kabul

TIBET

Lhasa

Chungking

Shikoko

Kyushu

East China Sea

Midway Is. (U.S.)

30N

Delhi

Katmandu

Punaka

NEPAL

BHUTAN

Hong Kong (G. Br.)

Hawaiian Islands

OCEAN

INDIA (G. Br.)

BURMA (G. Br.)

FORMOSA (TAIWAN) (Japan)

Macau (Port.)

Marianas Islands (Japan)

Wake I. (U.S.)

HAWAII (U.S.)

20N

Rangoon

Hanoi

FRENCH

20N

Bay

THAILAND (Fr.)

Manila

PHILIPPINES (U.S.)

Guam (U.S.)

Marshall Islands (Japan)

Bangkok

INDOCHINA

South China Sea (G. Br.)

10N

of

Bengal

Colombo

CEYLON (G. Br.)

MALAY STATES

BRUNEI

SARAWAK

Sandakan

N. BORNEO

Caroline Islands (Japan)

10N

EQUATOR

Sumatra

Singapore

Kuching

Borneo

EQUATOR

0

NETHERLANDS INDIES (Neth.)

New Guinea

NORTHEAST NEW GUINEA (Aust.)

Solomon Islands (G. Br.)

Batavia

Java

PAPUA (Aust.)

10S

(Port.)

10S

INDIAN

Timor Sea

New Hebrides (G. Br. & Fr.)

Fiji (G. Br.)

SOUTH

20S

OCEAN

Coral Sea

New Caledonia (Fr.)

PACIFIC

20S

AUSTRALIA

30S

OCEAN

30S

Canberra

Tasman Sea

NEW

40S

Wellington

ZEALAND

40S

Greatest extent of the Japanese Empire, 6 August 1942

⊛ National or colonial capital

(Neth.) Country in control prior to Japanese conquest

COLONIAL ABBREVIATIONS:
Aust. .... Australia
Fr. .... France
G. Br. .... Great Britian
Neth. .... Netherlands
Port. .... Portugal
U.S. .... United States
U.S.S.R. .... Soviet Union

0   miles   1500
0   kilometers   2000

60E 70E 80E 90E 100E 110E 120E 120E 130E 140E 150E 160E 170E 180 170W

banner with a blue star in the middle. That, I knew, was to show that a member of the family was in the Army or Navy. Around my neighborhood I had seen a few banners with blue stars. Now, I knew, there would be many more. And soon there would be gold stars, the sign that a son, daughter, husband, wife, or other family member had been killed in the war.

An announcer on the radio kept saying that all members of the armed forces should report to their bases. I heard footsteps on the stairs and looked out our front window. The mother and father from upstairs were on the porch saying

goodbye to their son. He had an Army Air Corps patch on the sleeve of his uniform. I watched him walk down the porch steps and head for the bus stop on the corner. He never came back.

The radio announcer said that Pearl Harbor was a U.S. Navy base near Honolulu, on the Hawaiian island of Oahu. I knew that the Hawaiian Islands were in the Pacific Ocean, more than 2,000 miles (3,200 km) from California. Hawaii was then a U.S. territory. (It would not become a state until 1959.)

Japan had an emperor named Hirohito, but the real rulers of Japan were the army generals and the navy admirals. They believed that Japan should become a powerful nation, with a big empire made by conquering countries in Asia. In 1931, without the knowledge of the emperor, the army took over Manchuria, which was part of China, and changed its name to Manchukuo. The army wanted Manchuria so that Japanese troops could be placed along what had been the Chinese border with the Soviet Union.

For many years, American churches had been sending missionaries to China to preach the Christian Gospel and convert Chinese people to Christianity.

Many American Christians gave money to priests and ministers in China. In my Catholic school, there were little coin boxes on the nuns' desks. We pupils put pennies, nickels, and dimes into those boxes to help the priests and nuns who were working in China.

Mostly because of the work of the missionaries, Americans got to know and like China. So, when Japanese troops invaded China again in 1937, many Americans turned against Japan. Parents stopped buying toys that had "made in Japan" stamped on them. Anger grew when Japanese warplanes bombed Chinese cities and a U.S. Navy ship. The newsreels—short news films shown between full-length movies—gave Americans horrifying views of bombs blowing up Chinese cities and killing Chinese people. My war cards also showed the bombings.

By the spring of 1940, Germany had taken over France and the Netherlands. Those European countries controlled colonies in Asia. France's colony was Indochina. The Dutch colony was the Netherlands Indies. Germany and Japan had signed a treaty in 1936 that made them allies in war. Because of that treaty, Germany let Japan take over the Pacific colonies formerly controlled by France and the Netherlands. The colonies had raw materials—oil, tin, and rubber—that Japan needed to continue its conquests.

Japanese soldiers who were already in China could march into Indochina. To conquer the Netherlands Indies, though, Japan would have to move soldiers by ship. To show U.S. anger toward Japan's conquests—and to warn Japan to stop making more conquests—President Franklin D. Roosevelt moved the U.S. Navy's Pacific Fleet from California to Pearl Harbor. When Japanese troops pushed deeper into Indochina in July 1941, the United States responded by cutting off all oil exports to Japan. That angered Japan. Army General Hideki Tojo took over as prime minister and told Japan to "get ready for war."

Admiral Isoroku Yamamoto, Commander in Chief of the Japanese Combined Fleet, did just that. The admiral, who had once lived in the United States, did not like the idea of going to war against the United States. But he believed that if Japan struck "a fatal blow" to the U.S. Navy's ships at Pearl Harbor, the United States, unable to fight back, would have to negotiate with Japan and allow it to keep extending its empire and getting raw materials from Southeast Asia.

U.S. Navy battleships ruled the seas of the 1930s. Here, the *Arizona* leads the battle line followed by the *Nevada*, *Tennessee*, *New Mexico*, *Mississippi*, and *Idaho*. In the background sails the aircraft carrier *Saratoga*. In World War II, aircraft carriers would become more important than battleships.

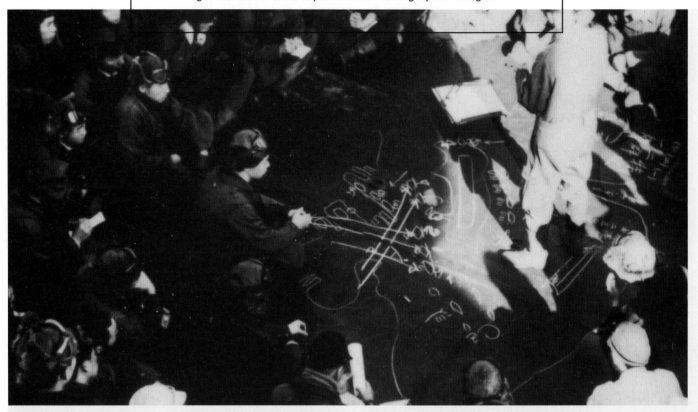

On a Japanese aircraft carrier an officer stands over a chalk drawing of Pearl Harbor as he gives last-minute orders to pilots. Arrows show flight paths to targets.

Generals and admirals sometimes plan a battle by playing a war game, with some officers making believe they are the enemy. The two sides in the game may move model ships around on a table and take turns making moves, as in chess. In September 1941, top Japanese naval officers got together to play a secret Pearl Harbor war game. In the game, the officers playing the United States sent out patrol planes that spotted and sank Japanese aircraft carriers heading for Pearl Harbor. But Admiral Yamamoto was the umpire of the game, and he said the carriers were not sunk. The planning for an attack by six aircraft carriers would go on.

Admiral Yamamoto knew that the U.S. Navy believed there was no way that a torpedo bomber could sink a warship in Pearl Harbor. The water was so shallow and the entrance to the harbor so twisty that ordinary torpedoes could not reach the anchored warships. A torpedo bomber needed a long, level approach to aim and release a torpedo, which then plunged at least 100 feet (30 m) down before rising and beginning its run to the target.

To train his pilots, Admiral Yamamoto sent an aircraft carrier to the Japanese island of Kyushu, which had a bay that looked like Pearl Harbor. At Kyushu,

Japanese pilots pose on the flight deck of the *Kaga* before takeoff on December 7, 1941. Among them are Yuji Akamatsu (fourth from the left, bottom row) and Haruo Yoshino (second from the left, third row), survivors who remember the Pearl Harbor attack in this book.

Commander Mitsuo Fuchida, who would lead the Pearl Harbor attack, laid out a course for pilots to fly—without telling them why. He also had them drop dummy torpedoes equipped with special wooden fins that kept the torpedoes near the surface.

One of the pilots, Haruo Yoshino, remembers, "We were told the altitude would have to be as low as 10 meters (33 feet). We never used altimeters. We flew totally by the seat of our pants. You could tell you were flying too low if the spray from the dropped torpedo could splash up and hit your wings."

"We trained fiercely, morning, noon, and night. We never had a day off, except when it rained," another pilot, Yuji Akamatsu, remembers. "And we knew that we were about to start a war with America. We were shown drawings of ships on large cards and told to learn them. Two of them were the *Pennsylvania* and the *Oklahoma*."

On November 26, 1941, Admiral Yamamoto ordered six aircraft carriers and other support ships to leave Japan and sail to Hawaii. Also heading for Pearl Harbor were many submarines, including five that carried midget submarines.

The admiral used a code to send the orders by radio telegraph. U.S. code breakers, who listened to Japanese radio messages, could not yet crack all Japanese military codes. But the code breakers did understand diplomatic messages that Japanese officials sent in another code to the Japanese Embassy in Washington, D.C. Special Japanese ambassadors were in Washington, talking with representatives of the United States. By cracking coded messages between Tokyo and the Japanese Embassy, the United States knew that Japan was talking in Washington about peace

Yuji Akamatsu

A Japanese officer tells bomber pilots the latest information about their target—Pearl Harbor. Pilots, who knew the dangers that awaited them, were told: "Win or lose, you will fight and die for your country!"

while getting ready for war. But where and how and when would the war begin? That was Japan's big secret.

At 5:30 on the morning of December 7, the Japanese carriers were 235 miles (378 km) north of Oahu. "The ships pitched and rolled in the rough sea, kicking up white surf from the predawn blackness of the water," Commander Fuchida remembered. "At times waves came over the flight deck, and crews clung desperately to their planes to keep them from going into the sea."

Pilots tuned their radios to a radio station in Honolulu. Using the station's American music as a guiding beam, they flew toward Pearl Harbor. "Our fighting spirit was high," says Haruo Yoshino, who was flying a torpedo bomber from the aircraft carrier *Kaga*. "There was no question in my mind that we would be successful. We really did not have much fear. We listened to the radio. The American stations were broadcasting normally. So it seemed they were not aware of anything. And that is when I knew that it was going to be a sneak attack."

The six aircraft carriers turned into the wind, and the first wave of planes—183 fighters, bombers, and torpedo planes—began to take off. On the *Akagi*, Commander Fuchida remembered, "Men lining the flight deck held their breath as the first plane took off successfully just before the ship took a downward pitch. The next plane was already moving forward. There were loud cheers as each plane rose into the air."

While a Japanese aircraft carrier rocks on a choppy sea, crewmen pull away wheel
chocks and crouch to keep clear of whirring propellers.
In moments the planes would take off for the attack on Pearl Harbor.

Midget submarines are lined up in a dry dock at a Japanese naval base. They were being built to attack U.S. ships in the event of an invasion of Japan. The invasion did not happen. A U.S. Navy photographer took this photo soon after the Japanese surrendered.

to ra, to ra, to ra

On the night of Saturday, December 6, Japanese submarine *I-16* came up from the sea a few miles off Pearl Harbor. Attached to the deck of the *I-16* was a midget submarine 81 feet (25 m) long. Kichiji Dewa, a member of the *I-16* crew, thought that the midget looked "tiny, like a bean." Kichiji Dewa's job was to help get the midget ready to go underwater and enter Pearl Harbor. Standing in the darkness on the deck of the *I-16*, crewmen could see the city lights of Honolulu and the lights that marked the entrance to Pearl Harbor. When the wind shifted, they could hear band music coming from the hotels along the shore.

"When I was in junior high school, I was taught by my teachers and others that Japan would make war with America," Kichiji Dewa remembers. "While being trained in the Japanese Navy, I learned about Japan's secret weapon, the midget submarine. It had two torpedoes, and only two men could get into it. Each torpedo carried about 450 kilograms (1,000 pounds) of explosives. Inside was real narrow. On the *I-16*, my assignment was the midget submarine. Sulfurous acid gas always came from the storage battery, and the gas filled the submarine. I was a maintenance man, and I had to keep the submarine in the best condition possible."

Kichiji Dewa

The *I-16* was one of five "mother" submarines that had carried midget submarines to the sea off Pearl Harbor. The five midget submarines were to slip into Pearl Harbor and attack the U.S. Navy's Pacific Fleet. The Japanese were especially interested in the U.S. aircraft carriers. If they could be sunk along with the battleships, there would be no way the U.S. Navy could fight—at least not for a long time. The U.S. aircraft carriers usually were moored along Ford Island, in the middle of Pearl Harbor. Also moored there were U.S. battleships and other, smaller, Navy ships.

The Japanese Navy knew just where the U.S. ships were, thanks to a spy. The Japanese government had an office, called a diplomatic consulate, in Honolulu. The spy was supposed to be a regular worker in the consulate. But he really was

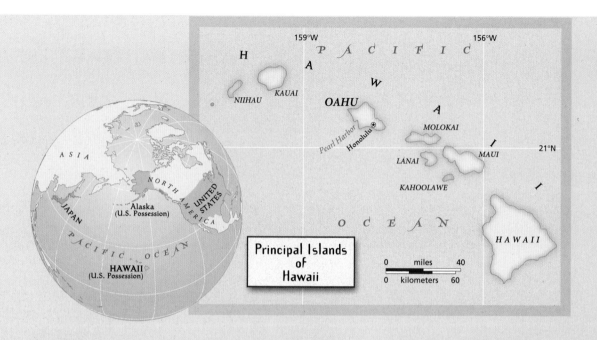

watching the U.S. Navy base and sending reports back to Tokyo. From Tokyo, the reports went by radio to the Japanese aircraft carriers.

The spy did much of his spying in a Japanese teahouse on a mountainside overlooking Pearl Harbor. Using a telescope from a window on the second floor, he could see the coming and going of ships in Pearl Harbor. He could also see and count the aircraft on nearby Hickam Field, where the U.S. Army had a big air base. (There was no U.S. Air Force yet; the Air Corps was part of the U.S. Army.)

U.S. counterintelligence specialists suspected that a spy was sending messages about Pearl Harbor, but they did not know who the spy was. And even if there was a spy, they did not think this meant that Japan was planning an attack. This was because Japanese officials were in Washington talking with American officials about ways to keep the two countries from going to war.

But the attack was now all but certain. Kichiji Dewa had known about the plan to attack Pearl Harbor back in October 1941, when special training began for the midget submarines. "We went to places along the coast of the Inland Sea of Japan, where there were bays like Pearl Harbor's," he says. "We trained to enter narrow places at night. And we worked in the day, too. So I was sleepy all the time.

"My diary says that on October 31, 1941, I saw a map of Pearl Harbor and learned about its geography. And then I knew that we were training for Pearl Harbor. We knew that the harbor was protected by anti-submarine nets. So the midgets were

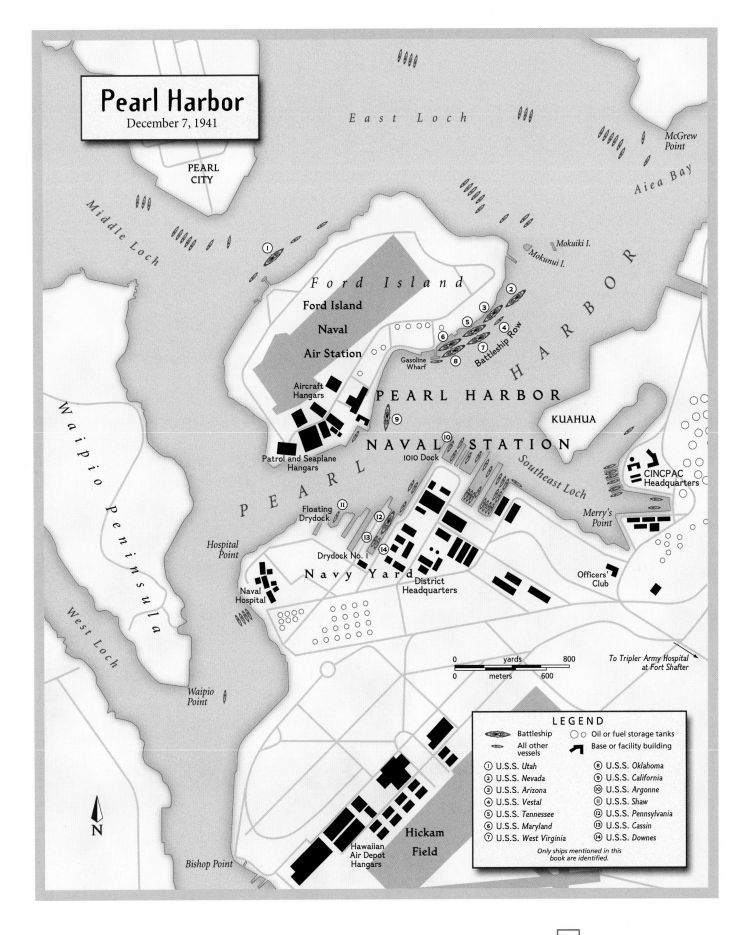

Pearl Harbor
December 7, 1941

PEARL CITY

East Loch

McGrew Point

Aiea Bay

Middle Loch

Mokuiki I.

Mokunui I.

①

Ford Island

Ford Island
Naval
Air Station

②
③
⑤
⑥
④
⑦
⑧

Battleship Row

Gasoline Wharf

H A R B O R

PEARL HARBOR

KUAHUA

Aircraft
Hangars

⑨

W a i p i o   P e n i n s u l a

Patrol and Seaplane
Hangars

⑩

NAVAL STATION

1010 Dock

Southeast Loch

CINCPAC
Headquarters

Merry's Point

P E A R L

⑪

Floating
Drydock

⑫

⑬
⑭

Officers'
Club

Hospital Point

Drydock No. 1

Navy Yard

District
Headquarters

Naval
Hospital

West Loch

To Tripler Army Hospital at Fort Shafter

| 0 | yards | 800 |
| 0 | meters | 600 |

Waipio Point

Hawaiian
Air Depot
Hangars

Hickam
Field

N

Bishop Point

LEGEND

Battleship ◍◍◍   ◯ ◦ Oil or fuel storage tanks

All other ◍◍   ◣ Base or facility building
vessels

① U.S.S. *Utah*   ⑧ U.S.S. *Oklahoma*
② U.S.S. *Nevada*   ⑨ U.S.S. *California*
③ U.S.S. *Arizona*   ⑩ U.S.S. *Argonne*
④ U.S.S. *Vestal*   ⑪ U.S.S. *Shaw*
⑤ U.S.S. *Tennessee*   ⑫ U.S.S. *Pennsylvania*
⑥ U.S.S. *Maryland*   ⑬ U.S.S. *Cassin*
⑦ U.S.S. *West Virginia*   ⑭ U.S.S. *Downes*

*Only ships mentioned in this
book are identified.*

to be underwater and follow American ships into the harbor. Each midget sub also had a wire cutter on its nose to cut the nets.

"My diary shows that the *I-16* left for Hawaii on November 18. The night before, we went to a special restaurant, where only officers could usually go. I was not an officer, but I could go with the men who would be in the *I-16*'s midget submarine, Masaji Yokoyama, the commander, and his crewman, Sadamu Uyeda. We ate, and we drank a Japanese wine called sake. Next day, we left under a clear sky. When the submarine crew learned that they would attack the United States, they were really surprised and got shaken. But it was no surprise to those of us who had trained in the midget submarine.

"During the day, the *I-16* stayed mostly underwater, running on batteries. At night, we stayed on the surface, running on our engine while we charged our batteries."

The midget submarine ran on an electric motor, powered by 224 batteries. The midget could run underwater at a top speed of about 20 miles (32 km) per hour. "I maintained the electric wiring," Kichiji Dewa says. "And I put in a special switch for the radio on the midget submarine. It would use the radio after it left the mother submarine."

The bow of a Japanese midget submarine shows its damaged cutter. The cutter, which looks like a corkscrew, was designed to cut the anti-submarine net across the entrance to Pearl Harbor. The submarine was found off an Oahu beach after the Japanese attack.

On the night of December 6, the *I-16* was on the surface, about 5 miles (8 km) from Pearl Harbor. Here are Kichiji Dewa's memories of the hours before the attack: "The mood on the mother submarine was calm, as usual. I went to the officers' mess, which enlisted men like me usually could not enter. We ate a farewell dinner. Later, there was a a small party in the officers' room. I didn't go to that.

"Masaji Yokoyama and Sadamu Uyeda each wrote a letter to his mother and father. 'Forgive this negligent son for not writing these long months,' Sadamu Uyeda wrote. 'Though harvest time has come and gone, you must be pressed with work this time of year. We are soon to be dispatched to regions unknown. Should anything happen to me, do not grieve or mourn. Should I fail to write, do not be alarmed, because it means I am well and discharging my duties faithfully. Goodbye.'

"Masaji Yokoyama and Sadamu Uyeda thought of themselves as closer than actual brothers. Sadamu, I remember, liked baseball. On that last night, after they crawled into the midget submarine, I communicated with them by a telephone on the *I-16*. I think they were a little nervous. We had an ordinary conversation about maintenance. And I told them, 'Take care.'

"The *I-16* went underwater and released the midget submarine. The midget was held to the mother with clamps. We let go of the clamps. Speaking on the telephone, I wished them success. I hoped that they would return. But Masaji Yokoyama said, 'If I come back, I'll come back with a wolf and put the mother submarine in danger.' So he knew that the Americans would follow them and get the *I-16*. And right away I began to miss them a little. I was thinking that they would not come back."

The Japanese attack was planned so that the submerged midget submarines would enter Pearl Harbor under cover of darkness. When the planes began their bombing, the subs would surface and fire their torpedoes. Before daylight the mother submarines went underwater. Kichiji Dewa and the other crewmen wondered what was happening at Pearl Harbor.

As the five midget submarines waited, the warplanes from the six Japanese aircraft carriers arrived. The most important targets for the attackers were the three U.S. aircraft carriers stationed at Pearl Harbor. But the spy's last reports had said that the carriers were at sea. So, at the last minute, the Japanese bomber pilots were told to aim at the battleships moored at Ford Island.

Japanese Air Assault on Oahu
December 7, 1941

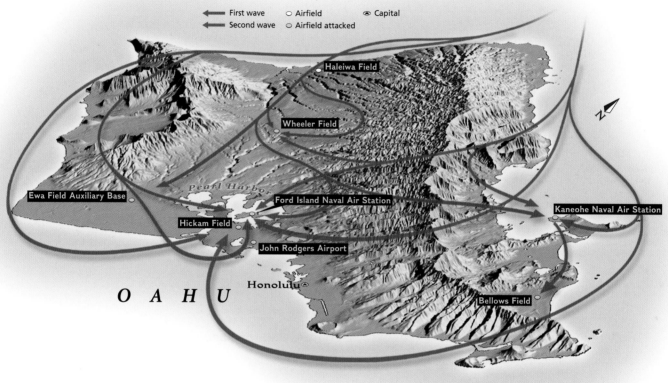

First wave
Second wave
○ Airfield
◉ Airfield attacked
◉ Capital

Haleiwa Field

Wheeler Field

Pearl Harbor

Ewa Field Auxiliary Base

Ford Island Naval Air Station

Kaneohe Naval Air Station

Hickam Field

John Rodgers Airport

Honolulu

O A H U

Bellows Field

On a day of peace in the 1920s, crewmen of the *Arizona* work around her 14-inch (35-cm) guns, which fired shells weighing 1,400 pounds (635 kg) as far as 20 miles (32 km). Before the ship became part of the Pacific Fleet, it was modernized.

The radios in the Japanese planes had telegraph keys, not microphones. The planes had to send messages back to officers on the carriers. Commander Mitsuo Fuchida, the leader of the attack, had his radioman tap out a signal: two short taps, one long tap, then two short taps (·· – ··). That signal—*to* in Japanese—meant "launch the attack." Then came three short taps (···)—*ra*—meaning the surprise attack was successful. Each signal was to be tapped three times to make sure the message went out. Because *tora* happens to mean "tiger" to the Japanese, the *to ra, to ra, to ra* telegraph signal unintentionally said "tiger, tiger, tiger."

In the first wave of 183 planes were 40 bombers carrying torpedoes. There were also 49 other bombers carrying armor-piercing bombs. They all were to attack the ships moored along Ford Island. The main targets were the battleships *Nevada, Arizona, Tennessee, West Virginia, Maryland, Oklahoma,* and *California.*

With their many big guns, battleships were the most powerful ships in the world. They had thick steel armor to protect them from gunfire. They had antiaircraft guns to fire at attacking airplanes. But they were big targets for bombers. Armor-piercing bombs could slice through the steel decks and then explode inside the ship. And a torpedo could sink a battleship by punching a hole in the underwater armor.

Battleships had been around a long time. Aircraft carriers were new and had not yet proved their importance in war. But the Japanese Navy's Admiral Yamamoto believed in carriers. He thought that airplanes from his carriers could wipe out the U.S. battleships and aircraft carriers in Pearl Harbor. Now, with no U.S. aircraft carriers to bomb, he had to be worried. Remember that war game? He knew that airplanes from the U.S. carriers could sink his carriers. And he did not know where the U.S. aircraft carriers were.

At 7:55 a.m. on December 7, the first wave of Japanese bombers swooped down on Battleship Row. Commander Fuchida sent out the signal: *to ra, to ra, to ra.*

Jinichi Goto, a torpedo plane pilot from the carrier *Akagi*, took his plane down to about 60 feet (18 m) above the water. He was surprised to see "the row of battleships in front of my eyes." Then, near him came what looked like little clouds. These were the explosions of bullets fired from the ships below. "Antiaircraft fire was heavy," he remembered. He dropped his torpedo. When the torpedo hit the sea, it dipped under the water and sped toward the battleship U.S.S. *Oklahoma*. The torpedo was one of the special type, designed to go down deep enough to hit a battleship at its most vulnerable spot—just below the waterline.

Haruo Yoshino looked down on Battleship Row. He, too, aimed at the *Oklahoma*. He dropped down to about 30 feet (10 m)—and remembered the lessons from his training at Kyushu: Don't go too low or the spray from the dropped torpedo will splash up and hit your wings.

"It was just as in practice," he remembers. "But right after I dropped my torpedo and turned to the right, I was hit hard by a tremendous sweep of machine-gun fire. Somehow I was able to get out of it. But the telegrapher-radioman behind me was injured, and his radio was broken. I then circled around the lower side of the harbor and out to the assembly point, where we gathered and then headed back to the carriers."

Haruo Yoshino

Yuji Akamatsu, the pilot who trained so "fiercely" at Kyushu, also piloted a torpedo plane. "We were aiming for the battleships," he says. "We flew over an airfield, low, and saw our bombers attacking. The hangars were aflame and the planes on the ground were burning. I saw American soldiers pulling hoses and riding bicycles and trying to put out the fires." Other Japanese planes—fast little fighters called Zeros—were zooming up and down the airfield, shooting their machine guns at the U.S. airplanes lined up on the runways.

Akamatsu aimed at a battleship and launched his torpedo. "It was all very precise," he says. "I didn't think about anything else. No matter what happened, I wanted to hit our target on the mark. And I did. Bullets filled the air from the anti-aircraft guns on the ships below. I saw four holes from bullets that hit one of my wings."

As Haruo Yoshino headed for the assembly point, he looked back: "There were seven planes of the *Kaga* torpedo squadron behind me. And five of them were shot down by antiaircraft machine guns. Fifteen men were lost, three in each plane. When I got back to the *Kaga*, my senior officer was under the bridge. He said dejectedly, 'We had terrible damage.' And because the American aircraft carriers were not there, it was hard for me to say that we had a big victory."

As Jinichi Goto, Haruo Yoshino, and Yuji Akamatsu flew to their carriers, another wave of Japanese planes reached Pearl Harbor. The second wave of 167

Battleship Row (see map page 21) from a Japanese plane: White lines in the center of the photo are tracks of torpedoes. At the left foreground is the *Nevada*. Behind her is the *Arizona*, with the repair ship *Vestal* moored at her side. Behind the *Vestal* is the *West Virginia*, which has just been hit by a torpedo.

While under attack, sailors at Ford Island Naval Air Station see a billowing fire cloud as the destroyer *Shaw* explodes. A sailor stands near the wings blown off a "flying boat," or PBY. At the center is a two-engine PBY still intact. Japanese warplanes destroyed 27 PBYs and damaged another 6.

Japanese Zero

bombers and Zeros mostly damaged ships that already had been hit. And once again the Zeros went up and down the runways of Hickam and other airfields, setting fire to planes on the ground.

One of the second-wave pilots, Iyozo Fujita, had not strapped on a parachute. If his plane were badly damaged, he would aim at a target and dive. Pilots called that "self-bombing." Most pilots had gone out without parachutes. They vowed to do what Iyozo Fujita planned to do but which he didn't have to do.

As he pulled up from strafing Kaneohe Naval Air Station, Iyozo Fujita was hit. So was a plane piloted by his friend, Fusata Iida. Iyozo Fujita saw Fusata Iida touch his mouth—a signal for fuel trouble. "I could see that gasoline was leaking from his plane," Fujita remembered. "He waved and pointed down and turned back." Through tears, Iyozo Fujita saw his friend dive on Kaneohe.

A few American planes got into the sky. Their pilots and the ships' antiaircraft guns and pilots shot down 29 Japanese planes.

The five midget submarines, each with a two-man crew, were supposed to come back to their mother submarines after the attack. None of them did. Kichiji Dewa and the other crewmen thought that all ten of the men on the midget submarines were dead. But one man was still alive.

Ensign Kazuo Sakamaki and Chief Warrant Officer Kiyoshi Inagaki were in a midget submarine that lost its way. The two men had thought they would both "die in battle," Ensign Sakamaki remembered. "Then something went wrong."

Kazuo Sakamaki kept trying to steer the little submarine. For 30 hours he struggled to get the submarine into Pearl Harbor. But it got caught on a reef. Kiyoshi Inagaki drowned while trying to swim to shore. Kazuo Sakamaki almost drowned, but he made it onto the beach near Bellows Field. An American soldier found him. Kazuo Sakamaki, ashamed that he had been captured, begged the soldier to kill him. Instead, he became America's first prisoner of war.

Kazuo Sakamaki

Back in the submerged *I-16* mother sub, Kichiji Dewa and the rest of the crew waited for news from their midget submarine. "I got a Morse code message that said, 'Successful surprise attack,'" he says. "They were supposed to come back and meet us after the attack. I heard the sound of depth charges. That sound remains in my ears to this day. No one came to the meeting place."

For the Japanese people, the nine men who died in the midget submarines became heroes. A painting of the heroes made them look like gods. Kazuo Sakamaki, because he had become a prisoner, was not made a hero. Kichiji Dewa remembers, "The submarine fleet held a memorial service for the midget submarine crews. At that time, I thought that there should be ten crewmen's pictures. But one picture was missing. Then I knew that Ensign Sakamaki didn't die and must have been a prisoner."

The midget submarines had not sunk any U.S. ships. But that did not matter to the Japanese people. They believed that their navy had won a great victory. One of the few Japanese officers to worry was Admiral Isoroku Yamamoto, who had planned the attack. He knew that the U.S. aircraft carriers were still in the Pacific. He believed that if Japan did not win the war very soon, it probably would not be able to win at all.

Freed from a reef, Sakamaki's midget submarine lies awash on an Oahu beach. Sakamaki survived only to become America's first prisoner of World War II.

Nine lost officers and crewmen of midget submarines are honored in a wartime painting as
"Nine Young Gods." In the center of the oil-on-silk artwork is the attack on Ford Island.
Missing is Kazuo Sakamaki, who was considered a disgrace because he became a prisoner.

These crewmen of the destroyer U.S.S. *Ward* had come a long way from Pearl Harbor when they posed with their "scoreboard" in 1944. On the morning of December 7, 1941, guns on the *Ward* fired the first U.S. shots of the Pacific War when it attacked a Japanese midget submarine.

CHAPTER 3 ————————

"this is no drill"

Early on the morning of December 7, the U.S. Navy destroyer U.S.S. *Ward* was patrolling the entrance to Pearl Harbor. After trying unsuccessfully to find a reported submarine, the *Ward* responded to a lookout's report of a *V*-shaped wave moving through the sea. He knew that a submarine just under the water made such a wave when it stuck up its periscope. Every man on the *Ward* ran to his battle station.

Ships had to enter Pearl Harbor through a kind of gate consisting of a heavy net that reached almost to the seafloor. The net was supposed to keep submarines from sneaking in. Thanks to the Japanese spy, the Japanese Navy knew about the anti-submarine net.

On the nose of each midget submarine was something that looked like a big corkscrew. It was supposed to cut through the net—a tough job. An easier way to get into the harbor was to wait until the gate opened for a Navy ship and then just follow the ship.

That seemed to be exactly what was happening. The gate was open, and the *V*-shaped wave was right behind the *Antares*, a Navy supply ship heading toward the gate.

Russell Reetz was at his battle station on the top deck of the *Ward*. "I was watching this object behind the *Antares*," he remembers. "I thought the *Antares* was towing something and that the whole thing was a drill. Suddenly, it rose out of the water, and I could see it was a sub. I saw not just the periscope but the whole conning tower." Then the captain of the *Ward*, Lieutenant William W. Outerbridge—on his second day as commanding officer—gave the order to pursue the submarine.

"All of a sudden," Reetz says, "the number one gun fired. But they missed because their elevation wasn't great enough—we were that close to the submarine. And then number three gun fired, and I saw the splash of the water at the waterline of the conning tower as the shell hit. Then we started dropping depth charges. I saw the depth charges drop off the stern of the ship. They were set to go off at 150 feet (46 m). They exploded, and a big gush of water came up. There were 250 pounds

Russell Reetz

U.S. Navy sailors haul a midget submarine from the waters of Pearl Harbor in 1968.
The five submarines were supposed to return to "mother" submarines after attacking Pearl
Harbor. But none of them made it back. Each carried two men and two torpedoes.

(113 kg) of TNT in each depth charge. So that would be 1,000 pounds (454 kg) of TNT exploding. It was so close to the submarine that I'm almost sure there was enough damage to sink it." (Another crewman thought he saw the midget sub—it could have been the one from Kichiji Dewa's *I-16*—roll over and sink.)

Although America did not know it yet, she was at war. And the *Ward* had fired the first shot.

It was 6:53 a.m. when the captain of the *Ward* sent a message to Pearl Harbor saying that his ship had attacked a submarine. A sailor on shore wrote down the message, which began to go from one office to another. The message, sent so quickly from the *Ward*, moved slowly toward top Navy officers.

Another warning came around 7:00. At six places on Oahu, Pearl Harbor's island, the U.S. Army had a new electronic tool called radar. The radar stations sent out signals that bounced off distant objects and returned, like a boomerang. Usually, the radars were turned off at 7:00 a.m. But at 7:02 on December 7, one radar station still was turned on for training. Soldiers at that station saw signals showing a large number of planes 132 miles (212 km) away—heading for Oahu.

The soldiers telephoned an officer at Fort Shafter. He believed that they had spotted some American B-17 Flying Fortresses on their way to Oahu. "Well, don't worry about it," he said. When he hung up, the planes were 88 miles (142 km) away. They were the Japanese planes, not the American ones coming in from California.

Around the time that the *Ward* attacked the submarine, it was Sunday noon in Washington. A long message, sent by radio, had been going from Tokyo to the Japanese Embassy in Washington. U.S. code breakers heard and deciphered the message. The message told Japanese diplomatic officials to stop the peace talks with U.S. diplomats at 1:00 p.m., which would be 7:30 a.m. in Hawaii. That meant Japan was planning a move toward war. But where?

Japan needed oil and rubber. So President Roosevelt and many other American officials believed that Japan was sending warships to the south. That would mean an attack on the Netherlands Indies or the British colony of Singapore. (In fact, Japan on December 7 would attack not only Pearl Harbor but also many other places in the Pacific, including the Philippines.)

A warning went out from Washington to U.S. generals and admirals in the Pacific, including the top officers in Pearl Harbor. The Japanese aircraft arrived at Pearl Harbor before the warning message did. U.S. leaders in Washington, along with the top officers at Pearl Harbor, made a lot of mistakes that day. As the war went on, they would do much better.

Around 7:45 a.m., Charles Christensen was in the crew's quarters of the U.S.S. *Argonne*, the flagship of the admiral who commanded the base. It was moored at 1010 Dock, across the harbor from Ford Island. "I was in my skivvies—that's sailor slang for underwear—and putting on my white uniform," Christensen remembers. "Next to my bunk was a small suitcase that I kept my roller skates in. Friends had introduced me to a young Japanese woman the night before. She said she liked roller-skating, so we made a date to go skating. I was supposed to meet her at 9:00 Sunday morning.

"An explosion slightly shook the ship, and I thought, Oh! That was a bad explosion! I wondered what had happened. And I opened the porthole and stuck my head out. And, oh boy, was there ever a fire on Ford Island! I thought, Wow! I'd better go take a look."

Smoke rose high over Ford Island. Out of the corner of his eye, Christensen saw a plane, low and turning. Painted on its wings were big red disks. "Meatballs," he and other Americans called them. To Japanese, they were the rising-sun symbol from their country's flag.

"I knew it was a Japanese plane, and the torpedo was underneath it," he says. "It's maybe 30 feet (10 m) off the water, which puts the pilot maybe eye level with me. I can see the man's face. He's got his helmet on. He's got his goggles on. And he's looking over the side. And when he straightened the plane out, he dropped that torpedo. And that torpedo went as straight for the *Oklahoma* as it could go.

"Shrapnel was just bouncing all over 1010 Dock. I tried to pick up a piece. It was still hot! I dropped it.

"The only time I got scared was when a high-altitude bomber came over and dropped a bomb. When you look up, you don't know that the bomb is traveling the same speed as the plane, and you think it's coming straight down. And I thought my time had come, right then. But where are you going to run? You just have to stand there and watch it. And it misses."

Charles Christensen

Blackening the Sunday morning sky over Pearl Harbor are clouds of oily smoke and puffs of exploding antiaircraft shells. The shells were timed to explode at certain heights. Small boats dart about, rescuing men from flaming water, as oil from the shattered ships catches fire.

George Smith

On the U.S.S. *Oklahoma*, George Smith was about to begin his fourth day of freedom after 30 days in the brig, as sailors call the ship's jail. "I was five foot three and, at the age of 17, the youngest sailor on the ship," Smith says. "My battle station was a loader on a five-inch gun, and I was so small I couldn't even pick up the shells. So they had me load the powder instead, because the powder bags didn't weigh as much.

"Well, I was young, and I disobeyed some orders. The captain put me in the brig and told me to read the *Bluejackets Manual,* the Navy's book on how a sailor is supposed to behave.

"Now, on that Sunday I was out, and I was getting ready for a day off the ship—liberty we call it. Then, over the loudspeakers I heard, 'All hands man your battle stations.' I thought it was another drill."

Many people on that Sunday morning thought that some kind of drill was going on. At a command center on Ford Island, Commander Logan C. Ramsey looked out a window to see a low-flying plane. A reckless U.S. pilot, he thought. Then he saw "something black fall out of that plane." A bomb! He ran across the hall to a radio room and ordered the telegraph operators to send out an uncoded message to every ship and base: AIR RAID ON PEARL HARBOR. THIS IS NO DRILL.

Three torpedoes slammed into the *Oklahoma.* "I was really scared," Smith says. "Then I heard 'Abandon ship.' The ship was already rolling over on us. We jumped into the water. It was only about a five-foot jump. I saw the ship and the big gun turrets coming down on me, and I began to swim as fast as I could.

"The ship rolled over. There it was, keel up. I was sure that many of my shipmates were trapped inside. There were a couple of other sailors still in the brig, which was set up in the carpenter shop. I found out later that when one of the torpedoes hit, it broke the carpenter's workbench loose, pinned the guard against the wall—the bulkhead—and he could not release the men in the brig. Everyone drowned.

"I swam around the *Oklahoma,* heading for the *Maryland,* which was moored alongside. They threw cargo nets over the side so we could climb aboard. But there were so many men from the *Oklahoma* on the *Maryland* that they ordered us to go into the water again and swim to Ford Island."

A civilian sedan races toward the smoking Kaneohe Naval Air Station. Although the ships at Pearl Harbor were Japan's main targets, airfields and naval bases were also hit. Honolulu neighborhoods were struck by "friendly fire"—U.S. antiaircraft shells that fell to earth and exploded.

Rescuers work on the capsized battleship U.S.S. *Oklahoma*, hoping to save men trapped inside. Some of these trapped sailors, standing in waist-high water, took turns sending SOS in Morse code by pounding with a wrench. On the afternoon of December 8, rescuers broke through and pulled out 32 men.

Dorie Miller receiving the Navy Cross

From Ford Island, Smith could see the great hull of his ship and rescuers trying to cut through it. "I couldn't stand looking over there, seeing my ship upside down," he says. "I cried that night. I kept saying to myself, What am I doing here? I could be home in Seattle going to high school with my buddies. I just quit high school to join the Navy—for this. I was scared. But I know I grew up that day."

Rescuers saved 32 men trapped in the hull. "And I have met all 32," Smith says. Many of his shipmates did not get out; 429 of the *Oklahoma* crew died.

Torpedo after torpedo struck the U.S.S. *West Virginia.* Bomb shrapnel tore into the body of Captain Mervyn Bennion, commanding officer of the *West Virginia.* Lying on the bridge and dying, he still gave orders. Mess Attendant Second Class Doris (Dorie) Miller and others lifted their captain and carried him to a first-aid post, where he died.

Then Miller ran to a machine gun. Miller, the ship's heavyweight boxing champion, was an African American, so he had not been trained as a gunner. All he— or any other black sailor—could become then was a cook or a kind of waiter called a mess attendant. He aimed the gun at a Japanese plane and began firing. "It wasn't hard," he said later. "I just pulled the trigger, and she worked fine." For his heroism, he received the Navy Cross, the first ever awarded to an African-American sailor.

Clark Simmons

Mess Attendant Second Class Clark Simmons remembers Miller as "a terrific athlete—baseball, basketball, football, swimming, boxing." Like Miller, Simmons was a servant to the officers. Simmons served on the U.S.S. *Utah,* an old battleship used for target practice. On Friday, December 5, after weeks of getting hit with 5-pound (2-kg) dummy bombs, the *Utah* had returned to Ford Island. The *Utah* was moored where the aircraft carrier U.S.S. *Lexington* had been—on the other side of Ford Island from Battleship Row.

On Saturday, December 6, Simmons left the ship for a "Cinderella" liberty—meaning he had to be back on the ship by midnight. On Sunday morning, he was awakened by explosions and looked out a porthole. "I saw a plane making a run on the *Utah*," Simmons remembers. "As he dropped his torpedo, the wing dipped, and he straightened up. The torpedo hit. And then came another plane and dropped another torpedo.

"Things were breaking loose. Furniture was sliding around. We heard the bugler blow the call for 'Abandon ship.' The ship was beginning to list when I was in the captain's cabin with two officers. We felt the ship lifting and beginning to roll over. We had picked up life jackets, but we didn't put them on. So, we could squeeze through a porthole about 18 inches (46 cm) in diameter and jump into the water.

"We began to swim toward Ford Island. They were machine-gunning us from two directions. I saw fellows yelling and screaming. I really didn't know what was going on. I got hit in the head, a shoulder, and a leg. But I got to shore, and a Navy medical corpsman gave me first aid. Every year, December 7 feels like my birthday. I feel like I was reborn on that day, because it was such a miracle I wasn't killed."

On Battleship Row, an armor-piercing bomb had stabbed deep into the *Arizona*, setting off more than a million pounds (500 metric tons) of gunpowder. The battleship exploded in a huge fireball. The explosion and fire killed 1,177 crewmen.

Carl Carson was a 19-year-old sailor on the *Arizona*. "I was out on deck doing the morning chores," he remembers, "when all of a sudden a plane came along. I didn't pay much attention to it because planes were landing at Ford Island all the time. Then chips started flying all around me. And I realized the plane was strafing me.

Carl Carson

"I could look up and see the 'meatball' on the wings. And I could see the pilot. I ran into the ship and started back to my battle station. The bomb went off. Afterward I learned that it had hit near turret number 4, where I had been working about 10 or 15 minutes before. I guess it knocked me out. I don't know how long I lay there. The water was knee-deep.

"A friend of mine was crying and asking me for help. I looked at him in horror. His skin was hanging off him. There was nothing in the world I could do for him.

"They gave us the word to abandon ship. And we just practically stepped off the quarterdeck into the water. I started to swim to Ford Island. I must have passed out and gone down in the water. Everything was peaceful and nice. It would have been so easy to just let go. And I saw this bright light, and something made me come to. And

there was oil all around. And fire all around. I had crude oil from the top of my head to the bottom of my feet and in my teeth. It tasted horrible. I still taste it today.

"The oil was all on fire all around me. A man saw me down there, and he reached down and pulled me up to the surface."

A boat came by, but it could not stop because of the spreading oil fire. It slowed down, and rescuers pulled men into the boat. Carson remembers getting to a hospital. He saw a shipmate dying there. "I wasn't bleeding anywhere," he says. "So I got up and walked out." Then the word went out for *Arizona* men to go to the *Tennessee* to replace that ship's dead and wounded. Carson went to his battle station, which was in the same place on the *Tennessee* that it had been on the *Arizona*.

Many small boats were moving around the harbor, saving men from the flaming water. Japanese airplanes flew low, shooting machine guns. On 1010 Dock, Charles Christensen and other crewmen began taking care of the wounded. "The oil was on fire," he recalls, "and they were trying to swim out of it. They'd come up and try to get their breath. The whites of their eyes were red. Their skin was coming off. To get them to the hospital, all we had was a dump truck and maybe three officers' automobiles. At the hospital, oil was all over everything and everybody. I never saw any panic. I was always proud of the Navy after that."

Torn by a gigantic explosion, the burning *Arizona* sinks. Several bombs struck her. The fatal armor-piercing bomb plunged through her decks and exploded in a forward magazine, killing most of the 1,177 *Arizona* men who died on December 7, 1941.

The second wave of Japanese planes—167 bombers and fighters—struck at 8:54 a.m. "They came down and machine-gunned us," Christensen says. "I'm standing there on the dock and, somehow, I don't remember being scared. I was excited. Everything was going off. Our guns were going off. And there were all the explosions over there on Battleship Row. I just couldn't believe all of this was happening in this short length of time. With all of these planes coming in, it looked like bees coming back to the hive. There were so many of them in there at one time it was amazing that they didn't collide."

People living only a few miles from Pearl Harbor could not believe what was going on that Sunday morning. "We were planning to go on a picnic," Claire Becker remembers. "I had married Paul Becker, a brand-new Marine first lieutenant in October and moved to quarters in Pearl Harbor. We had not yet settled in. We hadn't even put up drapes.

Claire Becker

"The sound of gunfire awakened me. I looked out the window and saw that the sky was full of gray smoke. Then a small plane—a Japanese torpedo plane—went right by the window. You could see the pilot, grinning a little.

"Paul got into his uniform and left for the Marine barracks. I turned on the radio and heard: 'Ladies and gentlemen, this is an air raid. Take cover.' The station played 'The Star-Spangled Banner' and then went silent.

"I went outside. I could see a little teeny silver thing in the sky. And then there was an explosion. I found out later I had seen a Japanese bomb drop on the *Arizona*, blowing it up. Then I saw the *Oklahoma* roll. You can't believe how fast a great big battleship can turn over."

Second Lieutenant Madelyn Blonskey, of the Army Nurse Corps, was in her room at the nurses' quarters near Tripler Army Hospital, which was about 6 miles (10 km) from Battleship Row. "About 8:20 a.m.," she remembers, "the on-call nurse in the operating room at Tripler called me, very upset and anxious. She said a soldier had told her Pearl Harbor was being attacked.

"I suggested that she go to the end of the operating room and look out. There was a good view of Pearl Harbor from there. She said to hold the phone. She returned shortly and said, 'Madelyn, something is strange. The sky is full of black smoke. There is an awful smell in the air, like burning oil, and a lot of noise.'

Madelyn Blonskey

"I finished dressing and went to the chief nurse and told her what I had heard. She was upset with me and told me not to listen to rumors like that. But I decided to go to the hospital, which was about a 10- or 15-minute walk away.

"As I stepped out of the nurses' quarters, I had an awful feeling. Usually, the smell of gardenias and hibiscus from the garden was delightful. But that morning I smelled the odor of sulfur and burning oil. I heard some buzzing above me. There were about 20 very small planes, flying low, almost touching the treetops.

"I hurried toward the side entrance of the hospital and started up the stairs to a second-floor porch. As I reached the top of the stairs—I will never forget what I saw—there were about 15 or 20 stretchers with injured men lying on them. They were lined up head to toe next to the railing of the porch. There were more bloody wounds—caused by shrapnel—than I had ever seen in my life. And nobody was with these patients. I asked a young soldier or sailor where he was wounded, and he said, 'Pull the blanket down.' His buttocks had been penetrated by flying hot shrapnel. I asked him if he was in pain. He said, 'No. Just numb.'"

Nurses gave the wounded morphine, a drug that eased pain. Too much morphine would be harmful. So, to show that a man had been given morphine, a nurse wrote the letter *M* on his forehead.

"We started operating," Madelyn remembers. "The air-raid sirens blew. And we heard the roar of planes over the fragile wooden hospital. We had nowhere to go. We had a patient in the middle of an operation. The big bombers, heading for Pearl Harbor, flew so low that the vibrations shook the instruments on the table.

"I was scared. I said to the surgeon, 'Colonel, I know God knows we did nothing to deserve this. And I am putting my trust in Him.' Then the last plane flew over and everything was silent. But about ten minutes later, we heard a tremendous explosion, and the colonel said, 'I wonder how many more casualties there will be.'

"Caring for the wounded and dying went on for days. Schools were made into temporary emergency rooms. The cafeteria was used for the operating room, and the kitchen was used for sterilizing instruments. There were shortages of bandages and medicines. We were not prepared for the many hundreds of casualties. But we did the best we could with what we had to work with. There was no shortage of blood. Civilians, soldiers, sailors, and Marines appeared day and night to give blood."

This B-17 Flying Fortress has just landed at Hickam Field, which was still under attack. Stripped of guns to save weight, 12 B-17s flew in from California on what was to have been a routine flight. Most managed to land intact. One landed on a golf course.

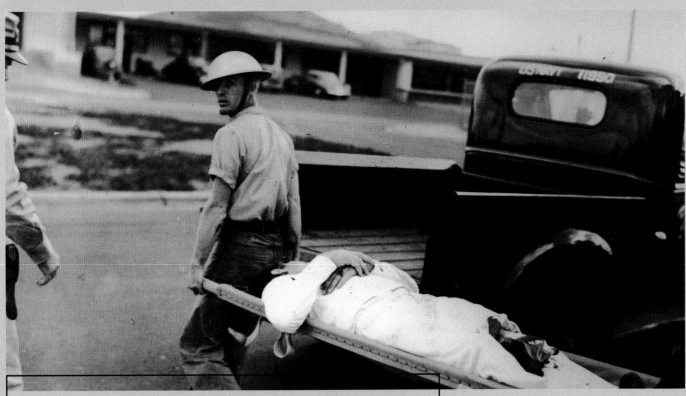

A stretcher bearer carries a wounded sailor to a pickup truck that will serve as an ambulance. So many sailors and airmen were wounded in the sudden Sunday attack that hospitals were jammed. Schools were turned into emergency hospitals, and at some hospitals patients were treated in beds set up on the lawn.

The Navy ordered survivors to send postcards like this one from George Smith. But the sailors were not allowed to describe the damage. Not until December 15 did the public learn that the *Arizona*, *Shaw*, and *Utah* were lost; the *Oklahoma* was listed only as "damaged."

On the night of December 7, thick black smoke still rolled across the harbor. Rumors spread that the Japanese were coming back to invade Hawaii. Antiaircraft guns were aimed at an enemy that was not there. Shells exploded, lighting the dark sky. When Charles Christensen looked across the harbor, he could see the American flag still flying on the sunken *California*. "We lived 'The Star-Spangled Banner' that night—'the rockets' red glare and the bombs bursting in air,'" he says.

For many days, only President Roosevelt and a few top officials knew the terrible cost of the attack: 2,390 Americans killed, 1,178 wounded. Thousands of mothers and fathers, knowing that their sons and daughters were at Pearl Harbor, waited and prayed.

Two days after the attack, the Navy passed out postcards and told survivors to write home. They were ordered not to describe what had happened on December 7. Seventeen-year-old George Smith wrote, "Dear Mom, I am OK. Don't worry."

"My mother didn't get that postcard until February," Smith says. "All that time she didn't know if I was alive or dead. When the mailman got the card at the post office, he closed down and ran all the way to my house. He woke up my mother and stepfather at 6:00 in the morning and told them, 'You're son's OK.' I would not see my mother for two and a half years."

Because the three U.S. aircraft carriers were not in Pearl Harbor on December 7, the United States could strike back. In June 1942, during the Battle of Midway, the U.S. Navy sank four Japanese aircraft carriers. Before the war ended in August 1945, the U.S. Navy would also sink the other two Japanese aircraft carriers that launched the planes against Pearl Harbor.

Out of the wreckage of December 7 repair crews built a comeback fleet. Except for the *Arizona, Utah,* and *Oklahoma*, every sunk or damaged ship returned to sea. When Japan signed the papers of surrender on September 2, 1945, the *West Virginia*, a symbol of Pearl Harbor, was among the U.S. warships in Tokyo Bay.

Lying in dry dock, the destroyers U.S.S. *Downes* (left) and U.S.S. *Cassin* (right) seem beyond repair. Behind them is the battered battleship U.S.S. *Pennsylvania*. On December 20 the *Pennsylvania* was ready for sea. Amazingly, the wrecked destroyers also sailed again the *Downes* in November 1943, the *Cassin* in February 1944.

In November 2000, Kichiji Dewa visits the U.S.S. *Arizona* Memorial, gazing on the wall that lists the names of the 1,177 men who died on the *Arizona* on December 7, 1941. Dewa's *I-16* submarine delivered a midget submarine for the attack.

CHAPTER 4

remembering pearl harbor

"Remember Pearl Harbor!" immediately became a war cry—fighting words that brought the American people together against Japan. Americans began singing a new song: "Let's Remember Pearl Harbor as we go to meet the foe. Let's Remember Pearl Harbor, as we did the Alamo...."

In 1941, Remember Pearl Harbor meant that Americans would go to war against Japan. Today we remember Pearl Harbor because we want to keep in mind what happened on December 7, 1941. Most of all, we want to remember the men, women, and children—both American and Japanese—and those days of war.

The remembering at Pearl Harbor centers on the U.S.S. *Arizona* Memorial. The memorial, made of white concrete, looks like a bridge that has come out of the sea. The memorial stretches over the sunken battleship. The remains of the *Arizona,* now in the care of the National Park Service, can be seen in the clear water.

At one end of the memorial is a wall on which are listed the names of the 1,177 men who died on the ship. Among the names are those of 36 sets of brothers and a father and son. The father, Thomas Free, died with his son William. Twin brothers Delbert and John Delmar were on board on December 7. Only John survived. Of the three Becker brothers (no relation to Lieutenant Paul Becker), only Harvey survived; Marvin and Wesley went down with their ship.

Another memorial is on a flat-topped hill in Honolulu, not far from Pearl Harbor. Its official name is the National Memorial of the Pacific. Because of its shape, people also call it the Punch Bowl. Buried here are more than 38,000 heroes who fought for America, from the Spanish-American War through the Vietnam War.

But the thoughts of survivors are the real memorials. When Kichiji Dewa came to the U.S.S. *Arizona* Memorial, he said, "I really started to question why we had to go to war. Japan and the United States should get along well to protect the world because

I think Pacific peace is world peace." Many American survivors come to the memorial and say much the same.

Japanese Americans have bitter memories. Even while the attack was going on, many Hawaiians accused Hawaii's Japanese population and AJAs (Americans of Japanese Ancestry) of siding with Japan. "Caps on Japanese Tomato Plants Point to Air Base," said the headline on one of several ridiculous—but hateful—local newspaper stories. Japanese fishermen were accused of sending spy reports to Japan.

Driven by two fears—that Japanese Americans would be disloyal and that Japan might attack California—the U.S. government rounded up nearly 120,000 men, women, and children on the West Coast. About two-thirds of these AJAs were U.S. citizens, and more than one-fourth of them were children younger than 15. They were taken to remote "relocation" camps in the western United States. They lived in tarpaper barracks, with a 20-by-25-foot (6-by-7.5-m) room allowed each family. They were allowed to bring only what they could carry. Barbed wire surrounded the camps, which were guarded by armed U.S. soldiers.

Not until early in 1943 were Japanese Americans allowed to enlist in the Armed Forces. In Hawaii, 9,500 volunteered, and about 2,700 were accepted. More than 17,000 Japanese Americans fought for the United States in World War II. U.S. citizens whose parents had immigrated to the U.S. from Japan became members of the 442nd Regimental Combat Team. Fighting against Germany, the 442nd became the most decorated military unit in U.S. history. The unit won 4,667 medals, awards, and citations. Other Japanese-American soldiers served in intelligence units. But when many of these brave soldiers wrote home, the address was a relocation camp.

In 1990, after years of delay, the United States apologized to the 60,000 survivors of the relocation camps and began paying $20,000 to each of them for their past suffering.

The memories, good and bad, live on at Pearl Harbor. But most of all, at the U.S.S. *Arizona* Memorial, both Japanese and Americans come together. In silence, they pray that never again will there be a Pearl Harbor.

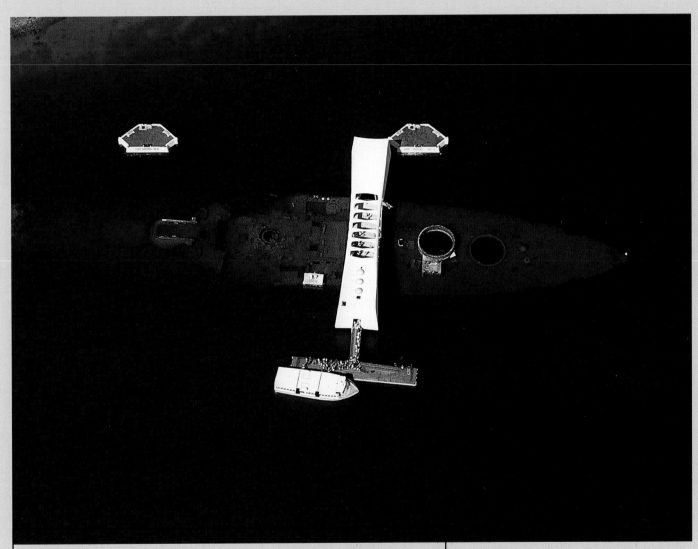

The white stone arch of the U.S.S. *Arizona* Memorial spans the sunken battleship.
She came to rest 40 feet (12 m) beneath Pearl Harbor on December 7, 1941. Each year, more
than 1.5 million visitors, many of them Japanese, come to this shrine of remembrance.

WAR IN THE PACIFIC

DECEMBER
The U.S., which supplies Japan with nearly all its aviation fuel, stops the export of technical information about the production of aviation fuel.

JULY
Japanese troops begin to occupy the French colony of Indochina. The United States responds by stopping its exports of scrap iron and steel to Japan.

SEPTEMBER
Japan, Germany, and Italy sign a treaty (the Tripartite Pact).

JANUARY
Japanese Admiral Isoroku Yamamoto begins planning an air attack on Pearl Harbor.

JULY
Japan pushes farther into Indochina; the United States cuts off all oil exports to Japan.

OCTOBER
Japanese Army and Navy officers say Japan should "get ready for war" against the United States. General Hideki Tojo becomes prime minister in a military-controlled government.

NOVEMBER
The United States tells Japan to get out of China and Indochina. Japan sends diplomats to Washington to try to find ways to avoid war with the United States. Six Japanese aircraft carriers and other warships secretly leave northern Japan and head for Pearl Harbor.

DECEMBER
Japan attacks Pearl Harbor. Almost at the same time, Japanese warplanes attack the Philippines and two U.S. islands: Wake and Guam, which are later occupied. Japanese troops also attack Hong Kong and soon after begin to invade the Malay States, Thailand, and Burma.

The day after Pearl Harbor the United States, Canada, and Britain declare war on Japan. Three days later, Germany and Italy declare war on the United States.

3:42 a.m. U.S. Navy minesweeper sights periscope off Honolulu Harbor, alerts destroyer *Ward*.

6:10 Planes begin taking off from Japanese aircraft carriers and head for Pearl Harbor.

6:45 *Ward* fires on submarine and drops depth charges. (It is near noon, Washington time. U.S. code breakers crack the last of a long message sent from Tokyo to the Japanese Embassy in Washington. The message tells the Japanese ambassador to break off peace talks at 1:00 p.m. Washington time. This is 7:30 a.m. Hawaiian time.)

6:53 In a radio message to Navy headquarters in Pearl Harbor, the *Ward* reports attacking a submarine.

7:02 Radar station on Oahu reports spotting unidentified aircraft heading toward the island.

World War II Timeline

This timeline highlights some of the events that occurred in the two main theaters of World War II: Europe (tan columns) and Asia (blue columns). A separate timeline for the hours of the actual attack on Pearl Harbor, December 7, 1941, (yellow columns), appears in the center, as this was the event that brought the United States into the war.

By the time the Japanese attacked Pearl Harbor, they had already started their expansion in eastern Asia. In 1931 Japan invaded northeastern China, setting up a Japanese state called Manchukuo. By 1938, Japan occupied much of China and had taken Nanking, longtime capital of China.

MARCH
Soviet-Finland war ends in Finland's surrender.

APRIL
Germany invades Denmark and Norway and will soon conquer both countries.

MAY
Germany invades and conquers the Netherlands, Belgium, and Luxembourg.

JUNE
Germany conquers France. German troops occupy northern and western France. Pro-German French officials set up a capital in Vichy and run the rest of France under Germany's watchful eye.

Italy, under fascist dictator Benito Mussolini, declares war on Britain and France.

Battle of the Atlantic begins as German submarines, called U-boats, begin sinking ships carrying oil and other war supplies from America to Britain. The U-boats will sink 3 million tons of merchant shipping.

AUGUST
The Soviet Union takes over Lithuania, Estonia, and Latvia.

SEPTEMBER
Hundreds of German warplanes begin bombing London every night for 57 nights in attacks that will continue until May 1941. More than 40,000 people will die in the "Blitz," as Londoners call the air raids.

Germany, Italy, and Japan sign a treaty (the Tripartite Pact) that makes the three countries allies against Britain and France. The treaty is also seen as a warning to the United States: Stop helping Britain and France. (The United States had traded 50 old destroyers to Britain in exchange for naval and air bases in the Western Hemisphere.)

OCTOBER
More than 400,000 Polish Jews are herded into a part of Warsaw known as the Warsaw Ghetto as part of the Nazi campaign against the Jews—the Holocaust, in which about 6 million Jews will be killed, along with hundreds of thousands of other minorities.

Italy invades Greece. German troops later come to Italy's aid.

U.S. flag flies over the U.S.S. *Arizona*

7:15 *Ward*'s message, delayed because of decoding, goes to office of Pearl Harbor naval commander.

7:20 The officer who got the radar report orders the station shut down. He believes the unidentified planes are U.S. B-17 bombers heading for Oahu from the U.S. mainland.

7:33 A warning message from Washington reaches a civilian telegraph office in Honolulu. A messenger picks up the message, which will not be delivered until after the attack.

7:40 The first wave of Japanese planes reaches the north shore of Oahu.

7:49 Commander Fuchida orders the Japanese aerial attack to begin.

MARCH
The United States begins "Lend-Lease," allowing President Roosevelt to send ammunition and other war supplies to Britain. No longer neutral, the United States now will give Britain all help "short of war."

APRIL
Germany conquers Greece and Yugoslavia.

JUNE
More than 3 million German troops invade the Soviet Union.

SEPTEMBER
German troops besiege Leningrad (now St. Petersburg). During the siege, which will continue until January 1944, more than 500,000 people in Leningrad will die of starvation.

OCTOBER
A German submarine torpedoes the U.S. Navy destroyer *Reuben James* in the North Atlantic. It is the first U.S. warship sunk in the European War. Only 45 of the ship's 160-man crew survive.

WAR IN EUROPE

AUGUST
Germany, under Nazi dictator Adolf Hitler, and the Soviet Union, under Communist dictator Josef Stalin, sign a Nonaggression Pact that secretly accepts Germany's plan to invade Poland.

SEPTEMBER
Germany invades Poland in a *blitzkrieg* (lightning war). Britain and France react by declaring war on Germany. This begins the European War, which will become World War II.

Soviet Union occupies eastern part of Poland.

NOVEMBER
The Soviet Union invades Finland.

DECEMBER 7, 1941

7:55 Japanese dive bombers strike military airfields at Kaneohe, Ford Island, Hickam, Bellows, Wheeler, and Ewa. Torpedo planes begin their runs on ships in Pearl Harbor.

Commander Ramsey at the Ford Island Command Center sends out a message: AIR RAID ON PEARL HARBOR. THIS IS NO DRILL.

8:00 The B-17s from the mainland reach Oahu, as do planes from the U.S. aircraft carrier *Enterprise*. In the confusion of the battle, both Japanese attackers and U.S. antiaircraft guns fire at the American planes.

8:04 Honolulu radio station KGMB interrupts music with: "All Army, Navy, and Marine personnel to report to duty."

8:05 Second torpedo hits battleship *California*.

8:08 High-level bombers drop armor-piercing, delayed-action bombs from altitude of 10,000 feet (3,000 m), hitting battleships and other targets.

8:10 Ammunition on the battleship *Arizona*, ignited by a bomb, explodes. The ship sinks in nine minutes.

8:17 The destroyer *Helm* speeds out of the harbor and fires at a midget submarine trying to enter the harbor.

8:39 The seaplane tender *Curtiss* and the destroyer *Monaghan* fire on a midget submarine in the harbor.

8:50 The badly damaged *Nevada* tries to get out of the harbor.

8:54 The second wave of Japanese planes arrives: 54 high-level bombers attack air stations and 78 dive-bombers protected by Zeros hit ships in Pearl Harbor. Bombs hit the *Nevada*, which grounds itself so that it will not sink and block the harbor.

9:30 The destroyer *Shaw* explodes.

10:00 Japanese planes begin returning to their carriers.

11:00 Fuchida flies over Pearl Harbor to assess the damage; returns to his carrier.

1:00 p.m. On the carrier *Akagi*, the decision is made not to launch a third wave.

1942

JANUARY
Manila, in the Philippines, falls to Japanese troops.

FEBRUARY
Victory in the Battle of the Java Sea gives Japan control of the Netherlands Indies.

APRIL
On the Bataan Peninsula, in the Philippines, U.S. and Filipino troops, low on food and ammunition, surrender. Japanese troops force about 76,000 prisoners to march to distant camps; at least 5,200 Americans die on the march.

Sixteen bombers, led by Lieutenant Colonel James Doolittle, take off from an aircraft carrier and make the first bombing raid against Japan.

The U.S. government forces thousands of Japanese Americans to move to "relocation" camps in isolated areas of the western United States.

MAY
U.S. warships in the Coral Sea turn back a Japanese invasion force heading for New Guinea.

JUNE
U.S. carrier-based aircraft stop a Japanese invasion of Midway, a U.S. base that guards Hawaii. The Battle of Midway is the turning point of the Pacific War.

Japanese troops land on Attu and Kiska in the Aleutian Islands of Alaska.

AUGUST
U.S. Marines land on Japanese-held Guadalcanal in the Solomon Islands. This is the first battle in an "island hopping" campaign that will keep moving U.S. forces closer to Japan.

SEPTEMBER
An aircraft launched from a Japanese submarine drops fire bombs on forests near Brookings, Oregon, in the first bombing of the continental United States.

OCTOBER
After months of desert fighting in North Africa, the British Eighth Army puts Germany's Afrika Korps to flight.

NOVEMBER
U.S. and British troops invade French North Africa.

DECEMBER
German troops near the outskirts of Moscow. Forced to fight in freezing weather, the troops pull back—defeated by the Russian winter, which had also defeated Napoleon's army in 1812.

1943

JANUARY
Japan's attempt to take New Guinea ends when Australian and U.S. troops defeat Japanese troops at landing sites. Australia is no longer threatened by invasion.

APRIL
U.S. code breakers intercept a Japanese radio message saying that Admiral Yamamoto is flying to the Solomon Islands. He is killed when U.S. fighters shoot down his plane.

MAY
The Navy announces that, except for the *Arizona*, *Utah*, and *Oklahoma*, all warships sunk at Pearl Harbor have been repaired and will return to sea.

U.S. forces retake Attu as Japanese troops evacuate Kiska, ending Japan's occupation in the Aleutian Islands.

AUGUST
A Japanese destroyer rams and sinks a small U.S. Navy vessel, *PT 109*, commanded by Lieutenant (and future President) John F. Kennedy. He and other survivors swim for five hours to reach a small island, where they are later rescued.

NOVEMBER
U.S. Marines land on Tarawa, an atoll in the Gilbert Islands.

FEBRUARY
German troops surrender at Stalingrad (now Volgograd). The Soviet Army, turning the tide of war, begins an offensive that will end in the capture of Berlin in 1945.

JUNE
The Royal Air Force and U.S. Eighth Air Force begin round-the-clock bombing of Germany.

JULY
U.S. and British forces land in Sicily.

SEPTEMBER
Italy surrenders. But German troops, continuing to fight the Allies in Italy, seize Rome.

NOVEMBER
The "Big Three," Churchill, Roosevelt, and Stalin, meet in Tehran, near the Caspian Sea, and pledge to fight together to defeat Germany.

1944

JUNE
U.S. Marines land on Saipan, in the Mariana Islands. Japan's last aircraft-carrier forces are defeated, as Japan loses 220 warplanes in one battle with U.S. carrier planes.

JULY
U.S. troops liberate Guam.

U.S. Marines invade Tinian Island in the Marianas. It will become a base from which B-29 bombers can bomb Japan.

SEPTEMBER
A U.S. Navy torpedo plane, piloted by Lieutenant (and future President) George H. W. Bush, is shot down near Okinawa. He parachutes into the sea; a U.S. submarine rescues him.

OCTOBER
U.S. troops land on Leyte, beginning the liberation of the Philippines. The Japanese Navy is so soundly defeated at the Battle for Leyte Gulf that it is no longer a serious threat for the rest of the war.

JUNE
U.S. troops enter Rome.

D day, June 6: 155,000 Allied troops under the command of General (and future President) Dwight D. Eisenhower, land on the beaches of Normandy, France, to begin the liberation of Europe.

AUGUST
French and American troops liberate Paris, France.

OCTOBER
British and Greek troops liberate Athens, Greece.

NOVEMBER
U.S. troops in Germany begin a drive to reach the Rhine River.

DECEMBER
German forces launch a surprise attack in the Ardennes Forest of Belgium, beginning the Battle of the Bulge (so called because the German drive put a "bulge" in the Allied battle line).

1945

FEBRUARY
Churchill, Roosevelt, and Stalin meet at Yalta, on the Crimean Sea. Stalin pledges to fight against Japan.

U.S. Marines land on Iwo Jima, in the Bonin Islands. It will be a base for fighter planes escorting B-29s flying from Tinian Island.

MARCH
B-29s begin bombing raids on Tokyo that last into the summer. Almost half the city is burned and more than 250,000 people die.

The U.S. Army liberates Manila.

APRIL
U.S. forces invade Okinawa, in the Ryukyu Islands—the islands nearest to Japan. Okinawa is needed as the base for the expected invasion of Japan.

AUGUST
B-29s, flying from Tinian Island, drop two atomic bombs—one on Hiroshima (August 6) and one on Nagasaki (August 9). At least 100,000 people die in the atomic bombings.

Soviet Union declares war on Japan (August 8).

Japan surrenders (August 14).

SEPTEMBER 2
Japanese officials sign the surrender document on the U.S.S. *Missouri* in Tokyo Bay.

JANUARY
In the largest land battle ever fought by the U.S. Army, American soldiers turn back German troops, winning the Battle of the Bulge.

Soviet troops take Warsaw, Poland, from the Germans.

FEBRUARY
The Big Three meet at Yalta, to discuss the division of Germany and other post-war issues.

MARCH
U.S. troops cross the Rhine River.

1,250 U.S. Eighth Air Force bombers attack Berlin.

APRIL
Vienna, in Austria, falls to Soviet troops.

Soviet troops enter Berlin and begin a street-by-street battle.

Italian guerrilla fighters capture and kill Italian dictator Benito Mussolini.

German forces in Italy surrender.

U.S. soldiers free 32,000 survivors of the Dachau concentration camp in Germany. It will become a memorial for victims of the Nazi Holocaust.

Nazi dictator Adolf Hitler kills himself.

MAY 7
Germany surrenders.

postscripts

For American and Japanese survivors of the Pearl Harbor attack, that day in December 1941 was the first of many days of a war that would not end until 1945 and that would affect them all of their lives.

Yuji Akamatsu and **Haruo Yoshino** were still on the aircraft carrier *Kaga* when U.S. dive bombers sank it during the Battle of Midway in June 1942. Yuji and Haruo survived the attack and went on to fight in different battles until Japan's surrender. After the war, Akamatsu went to work for an electric company, and Haruo started his own business.

Kichiji Dewa remained in the Japanese Navy until the end of the war, then he also went to work at an electric company, although not the same one as Yuji Akamatsu.

George Smith spent the rest of the war in the Pacific. After a few years as a civilian, he went to sea again—as a Coast Guardsman—during the Korean War. After the Korean War, he returned to civilian life, working at the University of Washington until his retirement.

Charles Christensen learned the machinist's trade in the Navy and went on to be a machinist in civilian life as well.

Russell Reetz was discharged in September 1945 after serving in the Pacific throughout the war. He went back to school and then into a career in refrigeration and air-conditioning.

Clark Simmons remained in the Navy after the war and later became a U.S. Marshal.

Carl Carson rose to the rank of chief petty officer. When he retired from the Navy in 1961, he became a farmer in Missouri. He died of cancer less than a year after making his first return visit to Pearl Harbor in 2000.

Madelyn Blonskey Knapp left the armed forces after the war and became an anesthesiology nurse in civilian life.

Claire Becker served in the Women's Air Raid Defense (WARD) in Hawaii until her husband received orders to return to the States in 1944.

Signpost along Waikiki Beach in the 1940s

Poster for a fund-raising concert to help build the U.S.S. *Arizona* Memorial

resources

WEB SITES

National Geographic on Pearl Harbor:
http://www.nationalgeographic.com/pearlharbor/

U.S.S. Arizona Memorial: http://www.nps.gov/usar/

Original documents on Pearl Harbor:
http://www.ibiblio.org/pha/pha/index.html

General information about World War II:
http://www.ibiblio.org/pha/index.html

Pearl Harbor Survivors Association:
http://members.aol.com/phsasecy97

Archives of Pearl Harbor investigations:
http://www.sperry-marine.com/pearl/pearlh.htm

President Roosevelt's Pearl Harbor speech:
http://bcn.boulder.co.us/government/national/speeches/spch2.html

BIBLIOGRAPHY

A Note about the quotes in this book: Quotes from Commander Mistuo Fuchida are taken from Paul Stillwell's book *Air Raid, Pearl Harbor*; those from Iyozo Fuchita, Jinichi Goto, and Kazuo Sakamaki are from Tom Allen's article in the December 1991 NATIONAL GEOGRAPHIC magazine; all other quotes are either from interviews the survivors had with staff from National Geographic Television in connection with its production *Pearl Harbor: Legacy of Attack* (available on home video) or this children's book.

Allen, Thomas B., "Pearl Harbor, a Return to the Day of Infamy," NATIONAL GEOGRAPHIC, December, 1991 (Vol. 180, No. 6).

Allen, Thomas B. and Norman Polmar. *World War II: The Encyclopedia of the War Years 1941–1945.* New York: Random House, 1991.

Hayes, Grace Person. *The History of the Joint Chiefs of Staff in World War II: The War Against Japan.* Annapolis, Md.: Naval Institute Press, 1982.

Hoyt, Edwin P. *Yamamoto: The Man Who Planned Pearl Harbor.* New York: Avon Books, 1983.

Layton, Edwin T., with Roger Pineau and John Costello. *"And I Was There": Pearl Harbor and Midway—Breaking the Secrets.* New York: William Morrow, 1985.

Lord, Walter. *Day of Infamy.* New York: Bantam Books, 1963.

Prados, John. *Combined Fleet Decoded.* New York: Random House, 1995.

Prange, Gordon W., with Donald M. Goldstein and Katharine V. Dillon. *At Dawn We Slept: The Untold Story of Pearl Harbor.* New York: McGraw-Hill, 1981.

_____. *God's Samurai: Lead Pilot at Pearl Harbor.* New York: Bracey's (US), 1990.

_____. *December 7, 1941: The Day the Japanese Attacked Pearl Harbor.* New York: McGraw-Hill. 1988.

Stillwell, Paul, ed. *Air Raid, Pearl Harbor: Recollections of a Day of Infamy.* Annapolis, Md.: Naval Institute Press, 1981.

index

educational extensions

1. What is the "foreword" of a book? How does a book's foreword add meaning to the text? Read the foreword of *Remember Pearl Harbor* and research its author, Robert D. Ballard. Why do you think he was chosen to write the foreword? What important background information did you gain about the topic?

2. How does the structure of the text contribute to the meaning and style? Describe the structure of *Remember Pearl Harbor,* including its use of illustration, photography, sidebars, and text. Give examples of how the presentation of information enhanced your understanding of the content.

3. How does an individual's personal experience enhance our understanding of history? Choose three personal accounts from the text and compare different perspectives on the war and happenings of the time. Distinguish between fact, opinion, and reasoned judgment. Analyze the relationship between primary and secondary sources.

4. In chapter 4, the author discusses differences between attitudes toward the "Remember Pearl Harbor!" slogan in 1941 and today. What conclusions does he draw? Use examples from the rest of the text and from personal experience to support or refute his claims.

more to ponder ...

- Why do authors write nonfiction? How can reading nonfiction shape our ideas, values, beliefs, and behaviors?

- What can we learn from reading real-life accounts of history? How are you affected when reading different points of view? How do the histories of earlier groups and individuals influence later generations?

- How has the world changed from the time period of the text? How do you think it will change in the future?

- Research a topic from the book. Compare and contrast information and details that you found from different sources.